Table of Contents

Please Save My Marriage

Sajjad Mundia

Please Save My Marriage

By Sajjad Mundia

Copyright © 2024 by Sajjad Mundia

All rights reserved. No part of this book may be reproduced, stored, or transmitted in any form without permission from the author, except for brief quotations embodied in critical articles and reviews.

Disclaimer: The information provided in this book is for educational and informational purposes only. It is not intended to be a substitute for professional advice. The author and publisher disclaim any liability arising directly or indirectly from the use of this book.

Disclaimer

The information provided in this book is for general informational purposes only. The author is not a licensed therapist, psychologist, or medical professional. The content within this book is based on personal experiences, research, and observations.

The practices, techniques, and advice presented in this book are intended to provide guidance and tools for self-awareness, personal growth, and emotional well-being. However, they should not be considered a substitute for professional advice, diagnosis, or treatment. Readers are encouraged to seek advice from qualified professionals regarding specific questions or concerns about their mental health or well-being.

The author and publisher of this book make no representations or warranties of any kind, express or implied, about the completeness, accuracy, reliability, suitability, or availability of the information contained within these pages. Any reliance you place on such information is therefore strictly at your own risk.

The author and publisher disclaim any liability for any loss, damage, or injury caused by the use or misuse of the information provided in this book. The reader assumes full responsibility for their actions and decisions based on the content of this book.

All product names, logos, and brands mentioned within this book are the property of their respective owners and are used for identification purposes only. Their inclusion does not imply any endorsement or affiliation with the book.

By reading this book, you agree to these terms and acknowledge that the author and publisher are not responsible for any consequences resulting from the use of the information provided herein.

Marriage is a beautiful journey filled with love, laughter, and companionship. However, like any journey, it has its fair share of challenges and obstacles along the way. Sometimes, these challenges can seem insurmountable, causing cracks in the foundation of even the strongest relationships.

In our fast-paced lives, it's easy to overlook the small cracks that appear in the walls of our marriage. We brush them aside, hoping they'll fix themselves with time. But as time passes, these cracks widen, and what was once a minor issue becomes a gaping chasm, threatening to tear apart the very fabric of our relationship. That's why it's crucial to address these issues head-on, before they escalate into something irreparable.

This book is a guide for couples navigating the maze of marriage, offering practical advice and wisdom to overcome common challenges and strengthen their bond. We understand that every marriage is unique, with its own set of joys and struggles. That's why we've curated a comprehensive list of topics, covering everything from communication breakdown to household chores, to provide guidance and support for couples facing difficulties in their marriage.

Whether you're a newlywed couple just starting your journey together or seasoned partners looking to reignite the flame, this book is for you. It's a testament to the power of love and commitment, and the belief that with effort and dedication, any marriage can weather the storms and emerge stronger on the other side.

So, let's start the journey together, armed with the knowledge and tools to navigate the ups and downs of married life. Let's bridge the gaps, embrace the challenges, and build a foundation of love and understanding that will withstand the test of time. After all, in the end, it's not about avoiding the storms, but learning to dance in the rain together.

Now, let's dive into the heart of the matter, exploring each topic in depth and uncovering the secrets to a happy and fulfilling marriage.

Bridging the Gap: Overcoming Communication Breakdown in Your Marriage

Communication—the cornerstone of any healthy and thriving relationship. Yet, despite its importance, many couples find themselves struggling to express their feelings or understand what their partner is saying. Whether it's a lack of effective communication skills or simply feeling misunderstood, the consequences of communication breakdown can lead to frustration, resentment, and even distance in your marriage. But fear not, because with some effort and commitment, you can bridge the gap and cultivate a deeper connection with your partner.

Understanding the Issue

Communication breakdown can manifest in various ways within a marriage. It might involve difficulty expressing emotions, conflicts arising from misunderstandings, or feeling unheard and unappreciated by your partner. Whatever the case may be, it's essential to recognize the signs of communication breakdown and address them proactively to prevent further damage to your relationship.

Listen with Empathy and Understanding

Practice Active Listening: One of the keys to effective communication is active listening. Instead of just waiting for your turn to speak, make a conscious effort to listen to your partner attentively. Show genuine interest in what they're saying, maintain eye contact, and ask clarifying questions to ensure you understand their perspective.

Validate Your Partner's Feelings: Acknowledge and validate your partner's feelings, even if you don't necessarily agree with them. Let them know that you hear and understand their emotions, and reassure them that their feelings are valid and important to you.

Be Empathetic: Put yourself in your partner's shoes and try to see things from their perspective. Empathy allows you to connect on a deeper level and fosters mutual understanding and compassion in your relationship.

Express Yourself Clearly and Respectfully

Use "I" Statements: When expressing your thoughts and feelings, use "I" statements to convey your perspective without placing blame on your partner. For example, instead of saying, "You always ignore me," try saying, "I feel ignored when we don't spend quality time together."

Be Honest and Transparent: Open and honest communication is essential for building trust and intimacy in your marriage. Be transparent about your thoughts, feelings, and needs, and encourage your partner to do the same.

Choose Your Words Wisely: Be mindful of your language and tone when communicating with your partner. Avoid harsh criticism, sarcasm, or passive-aggressive remarks, as these can escalate conflicts and hinder effective communication.

Practice Patience and Understanding

Give Each Other Space: Sometimes, it's okay to take a step back and give each other space during heated discussions. Allow yourselves time to cool off and reflect on the situation before returning to the conversation with a calmer mindset.

Be Patient: Communication is a skill that takes time and practice to develop. Be patient with yourselves and each other as you navigate through challenges and work towards improving your communication skills together.

Seek Professional Help if Needed: If communication breakdown persists despite your best efforts, don't hesitate to seek help from a couples therapist or counselor. A trained professional can provide valuable insights and guidance to help you overcome communication barriers and strengthen your relationship.

In conclusion, communication breakdown can pose significant challenges in your marriage, but it's not insurmountable. By actively listening, expressing yourselves clearly and respectfully, and practicing patience and understanding, you can bridge the communication gap and cultivate a deeper, more meaningful connection with your partner. Remember, communication is the key to a happy and fulfilling marriage, so invest time and effort into nurturing this essential aspect of your relationship.

The Money Matters: Navigating Financial Responsibilities

In marriage, one of the most common sources of tension and disagreement revolves around money matters. Whether it's deciding how to spend money, managing finances, or dealing with financial stress, the topic of money can often lead to conflicts and misunderstandings between couples. One particularly challenging aspect of this is navigating the discussion about sharing financial responsibilities. How can couples ensure a fair and balanced contribution without sparking conflicts? And how can they fill their lives with happiness while strengthening their understanding and love for each other?

Understanding the Challenge

The Money Matters arises when couples grapple with how to divide financial responsibilities fairly. It's natural for partners to have different incomes, financial priorities, and spending habits, which can lead to friction if not addressed effectively. Additionally, societal norms and personal beliefs about money can influence perceptions of fairness and equality in financial contributions.

Navigating the Discussion

Open Communication: The key to navigating the Money Matters is open and honest communication. Set aside dedicated time to discuss financial matters calmly and constructively. Approach the conversation with a spirit of collaboration and mutual respect, recognizing that you're both on the same team.

Define Financial Goals: Start by defining your shared financial goals and priorities as a couple. Discuss your short-term and long-term aspirations, such as saving for a home, paying off debt, or planning for retirement. By aligning on your goals, you can develop a clear roadmap for managing your finances together.

Understand Each Other's Perspectives: Take the time to understand each other's perspectives on money, including your attitudes towards saving, spending, and investing. Acknowledge any differences in upbringing, values, or financial experiences that may influence your views on money management.

Create a Budget Together: Work together to create a household budget that reflects your shared financial goals and priorities. Allocate funds for essential expenses, savings, debt repayment, and discretionary spending, taking into account both partners' incomes and financial obligations.

Agree on Financial Responsibilities: Discuss how you'll divide financial responsibilities, such as paying bills, managing accounts, and making investment decisions. Consider each partner's strengths, preferences, and availability when assigning tasks, aiming for a division of labor that feels fair and equitable to both parties.

Be Transparent About Income and Expenses: Foster transparency by openly sharing information about your incomes, expenses, and financial obligations. Avoid keeping financial secrets or hiding purchases, as this can erode trust and lead to resentment in the relationship.

Compromise and Flexibility: Be willing to compromise and adapt as your financial situation evolves over time. Recognize that circumstances may change, and be open to revisiting your financial arrangements periodically to ensure they remain fair and sustainable for both partners.

Fostering Happiness and Understanding

Navigating the Money Matters requires patience, empathy, and a willingness to work together as a team. By approaching financial discussions with openness and respect, couples can strengthen their understanding of each other's perspectives and cultivate a deeper sense of unity and partnership in their relationship. Here's how navigating this challenge can lead to greater happiness and love:

Shared Goals: Working together to achieve shared financial goals can strengthen the bond between partners and foster a sense of shared purpose and accomplishment.

Financial Security: Establishing a fair and balanced approach to managing finances can provide peace of mind and security for both partners, reducing stress and anxiety about money matters.

Improved Communication: Navigating the Money Matters requires effective communication and compromise, which can improve overall communication skills and strengthen the foundation of the relationship.

Mutual Respect: By respecting each other's perspectives and contributions to financial matters, couples can deepen their mutual respect and appreciation for each other's strengths and values.

Enhanced Trust: Openness, transparency, and collaboration in managing finances can strengthen trust and intimacy in the relationship, fostering a deeper sense of connection and security.

Conclusion

Navigating the Money Matters is a journey that requires patience, understanding, and collaboration between partners. By approaching financial discussions with openness, respect, and a shared commitment to achieving common goals, couples can navigate this challenge successfully and strengthen their bond in the process. By working together as a team, couples can fill their lives with happiness and love while building a solid foundation for their future together.

Navigating In-Law Interference: Building Bridges, Not Walls

In-laws. They're like that extra layer of family you didn't know you were signing up for when you said "I do." But sometimes, their involvement can tip the scales from helpful to... well, let's just say "challenging." When in-laws become a bit too involved in your marriage, it can stir up tension and friction between you and your partner. But fear not! With some thoughtful communication and boundary-setting, you can smooth out those wrinkles and foster a harmonious relationship with both your partner and your in-laws.

Understanding the Issue

In-laws can play a significant role in a couple's life, offering support, advice, and sometimes, a little too much involvement. Whether it's meddling in your decisions, criticizing your choices, or crossing boundaries, their interference can create strain and conflict within the marriage. This interference can stem from a variety of factors, including different cultural expectations, personality clashes, or simply a desire to be involved in their child's life.

Finding Common Ground

Open Dialogue: Start by having an open and honest conversation with your partner about how you both feel regarding the level of involvement from your respective families. Share your concerns, fears, and frustrations, and listen empathetically to your partner's perspective.

Set Boundaries: Establish clear boundaries with your in-laws regarding their involvement in your marriage. Be firm but respectful in communicating your expectations, and be prepared to enforce these boundaries if necessary. Remember, boundaries are not about shutting out your in-laws but rather about defining healthy and respectful interactions.

United Front: Present a united front with your partner when addressing issues with your in-laws. Let them know that you're a team and that you support each other's decisions, even if they may differ from what your in-laws expect or desire.

Choose Your Battles: Not every disagreement with your in-laws needs to be a battleground. Pick your battles wisely and focus on addressing the most significant issues that impact your marriage. Sometimes, a little flexibility and compromise can go a long way in maintaining harmony.

Communication is Key

Express Your Feelings: Be honest with your in-laws about how their actions or comments make you feel. Use "I" statements to express your emotions without placing blame, and offer specific examples to illustrate your concerns.

Listen Actively: Practice active listening when communicating with your in-laws, showing empathy and understanding for their perspective even if you don't necessarily agree with it. Validate their feelings and experiences, and seek common ground where possible.

Seek Compromise: Look for areas of compromise and common ground when addressing issues with your in-laws. Be willing to find solutions that meet both your needs and theirs, fostering a spirit of cooperation and understanding.

Fostering Happiness and Understanding

Navigating in-law interference can be a delicate dance, but with patience, empathy, and clear communication, it's possible to find a harmonious balance that respects the needs and boundaries of all involved. Here's how:

Strengthened Partnership: By presenting a united front with your partner and supporting each other's boundaries, you can strengthen your partnership and deepen your connection.

Healthy Boundaries: Establishing clear boundaries with your in-laws creates a sense of safety and security within your marriage, allowing you to focus on building a strong and resilient relationship.

Respectful Relationships: By communicating openly and respectfully with your in-laws, you can cultivate a positive and mutually supportive relationship that enriches your lives rather than causing tension and conflict.

Increased Understanding: Through open dialogue and active listening, you and your in-laws can gain a deeper understanding of each other's perspectives and motivations, fostering empathy and compassion.

Greater Happiness: By addressing in-law interference and fostering healthy communication and boundaries, you can create a more harmonious and fulfilling marital relationship, filled with love, understanding, and happiness.

Conclusion

In-law interference can be a challenging aspect of marriage, but with patience, communication, and boundary-setting, it's possible to navigate these complexities and foster a relationship that honors the needs and boundaries of all involved. By working together as a team, you and your partner can overcome in-law interference and create a supportive and fulfilling marital relationship that brings happiness and joy to both of your lives.

Embracing Appreciation: Nurturing Love and Recognition

In marriage, feeling appreciated and valued is like the warm sun on a chilly day—it's essential for growth and happiness. Yet, it's not uncommon for couples to find themselves in a rut where one or both partners feel like their efforts go unnoticed or unappreciated. When this lack of appreciation creeps into a relationship, it can sow seeds of discontent and disconnect. But fret not! With a sprinkle of gratitude and a dash of acknowledgment, couples can cultivate a garden of love and understanding that blooms with happiness and fulfillment.

Understanding the Issue

The feeling of not being appreciated can stem from various sources. Sometimes, it's a result of busy schedules and hectic routines that leave little time for expressing gratitude. Other times, it may be due to differences in communication styles or a lack of awareness about the importance of acknowledgment in a relationship. Whatever the cause, feeling unappreciated can lead to feelings of resentment, loneliness, and disconnection between partners.

Fostering Appreciation

Express Gratitude: Take the time to express gratitude for your partner's efforts, no matter how small. A simple "thank you" or a heartfelt acknowledgment can go a long way in making your partner feel valued and appreciated.

Notice the Little Things: Pay attention to the little things your partner does for you and your relationship. Whether it's making your favorite meal or offering a listening ear after a long day, these small gestures deserve recognition and appreciation.

Celebrate Achievements: Celebrate your partner's achievements, both big and small. Whether it's a promotion at work or a personal milestone, take the time to acknowledge their accomplishments and show your support and pride.

Show Affection: Show affection and love towards your partner in words and actions. Let them know how much they mean to you and how grateful you are to have them in your life.

Open Communication

Share Your Feelings: If you're feeling unappreciated in your relationship, don't be afraid to communicate your feelings to your partner. Approach the conversation with empathy and understanding, focusing on expressing your own emotions rather than blaming your partner.

Listen with Empathy: Listen to your partner's perspective with empathy and understanding. They may not be aware of how their actions—or lack thereof—affect you, so it's essential to approach the conversation with an open mind and a willingness to understand.

Find Solutions Together: Work together with your partner to find solutions that address the lack of appreciation in your relationship. Brainstorm ideas for how you can show more gratitude and acknowledgment towards each other, and commit to making positive changes moving forward.

Nurturing Happiness and Understanding

By embracing appreciation and acknowledgment in their relationship, couples can foster happiness, understanding, and love. Here's how:

Strengthened Connection: Expressing gratitude and appreciation towards each other strengthens the emotional bond between partners, fostering a deeper connection and intimacy in the relationship.

Increased Happiness: Feeling appreciated and valued by your partner boosts feelings of happiness and fulfillment, creating a positive and nurturing environment for both partners to thrive.

Enhanced Communication: Openly communicating about feelings of appreciation and acknowledgment promotes healthy communication habits in the relationship, making it easier to address issues and conflicts constructively.

Deeper Understanding: Expressing gratitude and acknowledgment towards each other deepens the understanding and empathy between partners, fostering a sense of mutual respect and support.

Stronger Love: By prioritizing appreciation and acknowledgment in their relationship, couples can strengthen their love and commitment to each other, creating a lasting foundation for a fulfilling and happy marriage.

Conclusion

In the journey of marriage, appreciation is like water to a plant—it nourishes and sustains the relationship, allowing it to flourish and grow. By embracing appreciation and acknowledgment in their relationship, couples can nurture happiness, understanding, and love, creating a strong and resilient bond that withstands the test of time. So, take the time to express gratitude for your partner's efforts, and watch as your relationship blossoms with happiness and fulfillment.

Navigating Career Conflicts: Finding Harmony Between Work and Family

In the hustle and bustle of modern life, finding a balance between our career aspirations and family commitments can feel like trying to juggle too many balls at once. Career conflicts arise when the demands of work encroach upon precious time with family, causing strain and tension in our relationships. But fear not! With a little mindfulness, communication, and prioritization, couples can navigate these challenges and find a harmonious balance that fills their lives with happiness and strengthens their love for each other.

Understanding the Issue

Career conflicts stem from the clash between the demands of our professional lives and the desire to nurture our relationships and spend quality time with our loved ones. Whether it's long hours at the office, frequent business trips, or the pressure to excel in our careers, these demands can often leave little time and energy for our families, leading to feelings of neglect and resentment.

Finding Balance

Prioritize Family Time: Make a conscious effort to prioritize family time amidst your busy schedule. Set aside dedicated time each day or week to spend quality time with your partner and children, whether it's sharing a meal together, going for a walk, or simply engaging in meaningful conversations.

Set Boundaries: Establish clear boundaries between your work life and your family life to prevent work from encroaching upon your personal time. Avoid checking work emails or taking calls during family time, and communicate your boundaries to your employer and colleagues to ensure they respect your time outside of work.

Delegate and Outsource: Delegate tasks and responsibilities at work whenever possible to free up time and energy for your family. Similarly, consider outsourcing household chores or errands to lighten the load and create more opportunities for quality time with your loved ones.

Communicate Openly: Communicate openly with your partner about your career aspirations, commitments, and the challenges you face in balancing work and family life. Be honest about your needs and limitations, and work together to find solutions that prioritize your relationship and family.

Supporting Each Other

Be Flexible: Be flexible and understanding towards each other's career aspirations and commitments. Recognize that both partners may have career goals and responsibilities that require time and attention, and find ways to support each other in achieving these goals while also nurturing your relationship.

Share Responsibilities: Share responsibilities and tasks related to managing both your careers and your family life. Work together as a team to divide household chores, childcare duties, and other responsibilities in a way that feels fair and equitable to both partners.

Celebrate Achievements: Celebrate each other's career achievements and milestones, no matter how big or small. Show your support and pride for your partner's accomplishments, and celebrate them together as a couple.

Fostering Happiness and Understanding

By prioritizing their relationship and finding a balance between work and family life, couples can fill their lives with happiness and strengthen their love for each other. Here's how:

Quality Time: Spending quality time together as a couple and as a family strengthens your bond and deepens your connection, fostering happiness and fulfillment in your relationship.

Open Communication: Communicating openly and honestly about your needs, aspirations, and challenges strengthens your relationship and promotes understanding and empathy between partners.

Mutual Support: Supporting each other in achieving your career goals and aspirations creates a sense of teamwork and partnership, strengthening your bond and increasing your sense of fulfillment and happiness as a couple.

Shared Responsibilities: Sharing responsibilities and tasks related to managing both your careers and your family life promotes a sense of equality and partnership, reducing stress and tension in your relationship and fostering happiness and harmony.

Conclusion

Balancing work and family life can be a challenge, but with mindfulness, communication, and prioritization, couples can navigate career conflicts and find a harmonious balance that fills their lives with happiness and strengthens their love for each other. By prioritizing their relationship, supporting each other's career aspirations, and finding ways to spend quality time together, couples can create a fulfilling and meaningful life together, where love and understanding flourish.

Navigating Jealousy and Trust Issues: Building a Foundation of Security and Understanding

In marriage, jealousy and trust issues can cast a shadow over even the strongest relationships. Feeling insecure or doubting your partner's fidelity can chip away at the foundation of trust, causing tension and strain between couples. But fret not! With a sprinkle of understanding, a dash of empathy, and a whole lot of communication, couples can navigate these challenges and strengthen their bond, filling their lives with happiness and love.

Understanding the Issue

Jealousy and trust issues often stem from feelings of insecurity, past experiences, or unresolved emotional wounds. Whether it's comparing oneself to others, fearing abandonment, or struggling with past betrayals, these feelings can create a rift in the relationship and undermine the trust between partners.

Building Trust

Open Communication: Start by having an open and honest conversation with your partner about your feelings of jealousy and insecurity. Express your concerns calmly and without accusations, and listen empathetically to your partner's perspective.

Establish Boundaries: Set clear boundaries with your partner regarding what is and isn't acceptable behavior in the relationship. Discuss what actions or behaviors trigger feelings of jealousy or insecurity and work together to find solutions that respect each other's boundaries.

Practice Transparency: Practice transparency and honesty in your relationship by being open about your feelings, actions, and intentions. Keep communication lines open and avoid secrecy or hiding information from your partner, as this can erode trust and fuel feelings of jealousy.

Build Self-Confidence: Work on building your self-confidence and self-worth independent of your relationship. Focus on your strengths, accomplishments, and positive qualities, and cultivate a sense of self-assurance that isn't reliant on external validation from your partner.

Managing Jealousy

Challenge Negative Thoughts: Challenge negative thoughts and beliefs that fuel feelings of jealousy and insecurity. Instead of jumping to conclusions or assuming the worst, consider alternative explanations and interpretations of your partner's behavior.

Practice Mindfulness: Practice mindfulness and self-awareness to become more attuned to your emotions and reactions. Learn to recognize when feelings of jealousy arise and take steps to calm yourself before reacting impulsively.

Focus on the Present: Focus on the present moment and the reality of your relationship rather than dwelling on past betrayals or hypothetical scenarios. Let go of the need to control or monitor your partner's actions and instead focus on building trust and connection in the here and now.

Rebuilding Trust

Consistency: Consistency is key to rebuilding trust in a relationship. Demonstrate through your actions that you are trustworthy and reliable, and follow through on your commitments and promises to your partner.

Forgiveness: Practice forgiveness and let go of past grievances or betrayals that may be contributing to feelings of mistrust. Holding onto resentment or bitterness only serves to prolong the pain and hinder the healing process.

Seek Support: Seek support from a trusted friend, family member, or therapist to help you work through feelings of jealousy and rebuild trust in your relationship. A neutral third party can offer perspective and guidance as you navigate these challenging emotions.

Fostering Happiness and Understanding

By addressing jealousy and trust issues with empathy, communication, and a commitment to building trust, couples can fill their lives with happiness and strengthen their love for each other. Here's how:

Deepened Understanding: By openly discussing feelings of jealousy and insecurity, couples can deepen their understanding of each other's perspectives and experiences, fostering empathy and compassion in the relationship.

Strengthened Trust: By practicing transparency, consistency, and forgiveness, couples can rebuild trust in their relationship and create a foundation of security and stability that strengthens their bond.

Increased Communication: Open and honest communication about feelings of jealousy and insecurity promotes healthy communication habits in the relationship, making it easier to address issues and conflicts constructively.

Enhanced Connection: By working through jealousy and trust issues together, couples can strengthen their connection and intimacy, creating a deeper and more fulfilling relationship based on mutual trust and understanding.

Conclusion

Jealousy and trust issues can be challenging to navigate, but with empathy, communication, and a commitment to building trust, couples can overcome these obstacles and strengthen their bond. By addressing underlying insecurities, practicing transparency and forgiveness, and seeking support when needed, couples can fill their lives with happiness and love, creating a relationship built on trust, understanding, and mutual respect.

Navigating Sexual Intimacy: Embracing Differences with Love and Understanding

In the journey of marriage, sexual intimacy is a vital thread that weaves couples closer together. However, differing desires or preferences in the bedroom can sometimes create ripples of frustration and discord. Fear not, for in the realm of love, there exists boundless room for understanding, compromise, and growth. By embracing open communication, empathy, and a willingness to explore, couples can transform their intimate lives into a harmonious symphony of love and connection.

Understanding the Issue

Sexual intimacy is a deeply personal and nuanced aspect of marriage, shaped by individual desires, preferences, and experiences. Differences in sexual desires or preferences can arise due to a variety of factors, including upbringing, past experiences, and physical or emotional needs. These differences, if left unaddressed, can lead to feelings of frustration, dissatisfaction, and disconnect in the relationship.

Embracing Open Communication

Create a Safe Space: Foster an environment of trust and openness where both partners feel comfortable expressing their desires, fears, and concerns without fear of judgment or rejection.

Initiate Honest Conversations: Initiate honest and respectful conversations about your sexual desires, preferences, and boundaries. Share your thoughts and feelings openly, and encourage your partner to do the same.

Listen with Empathy: Listen to your partner's perspective with empathy and understanding, seeking to understand their needs and desires without judgment or criticism.

Explore Together: Explore new experiences, techniques, and fantasies together as a couple, keeping an open mind and a spirit of adventure. By exploring together, you can discover new ways to connect and deepen your intimacy.

Finding Compromise

Focus on Connection: Shift the focus of sexual intimacy from performance or specific acts to connection and pleasure. Emphasize the importance of emotional connection, affection, and intimacy in your sexual encounters.

Seek Compromise: Seek compromise and find creative solutions that honor both partners' desires and preferences. Explore alternative ways to express intimacy and pleasure that meet both partners' needs.

Be Flexible: Be flexible and willing to adapt to each other's changing desires and preferences over time. Recognize that sexual intimacy is fluid and dynamic, and be open to adjusting your expectations and approaches accordingly.

Nurturing Happiness and Understanding

By addressing differences in sexual desires and preferences with empathy, communication, and a willingness to explore, couples can fill their lives with happiness and strengthen their love for each other. Here's how:

Deepened Connection: By openly discussing sexual desires and preferences, couples can deepen their emotional connection and intimacy, fostering a greater sense of closeness and understanding.

Increased Satisfaction: By finding compromise and exploring new experiences together, couples can increase their sexual satisfaction and fulfillment, leading to greater overall happiness in the relationship.

Enhanced Communication: Open and honest communication about sexual intimacy promotes healthy communication habits in the relationship, making it easier to address issues and conflicts constructively.

Strengthened Bond: By working together to navigate differences in sexual desires and preferences, couples can strengthen their bond and create a relationship that is grounded in mutual respect, understanding, and love.

Conclusion

Sexual intimacy is a beautiful and important aspect of marriage, but it can also be a source of frustration and discord if not approached with empathy, communication, and understanding. By embracing open communication, seeking compromise, and exploring new experiences together, couples can transform their intimate lives into a source of happiness, fulfillment, and connection. With love as their guide, couples can navigate the complexities of sexual intimacy with grace and compassion, deepening their bond and strengthening their love for each other.

Navigating Parenting Styles: Cultivating Harmony in Child-Rearing

In the symphony of marriage, parenting styles can sometimes create discordant notes, leading to arguments and tension between spouses. When partners don't see eye-to-eye on how to raise their children, it can stir up feelings of frustration, confusion, and resentment. But fret not! With a blend of understanding, compromise, and effective communication, couples can harmonize their parenting styles and cultivate an environment of love, support, and unity within their family.

Understanding the Issue

Parenting styles are deeply rooted in our upbringing, beliefs, and cultural backgrounds. It's not uncommon for spouses to have different approaches to discipline, education, and nurturing based on their own experiences and values. These differences can lead to disagreements and conflicts as couples navigate the complex terrain of child-rearing.

Embracing Open Communication

Create a Safe Space: Foster an environment of trust and openness where both partners feel comfortable expressing their thoughts, concerns, and parenting preferences without fear of judgment or criticism.

Initiate Honest Conversations: Initiate honest and respectful conversations about your parenting styles, beliefs, and values. Share your thoughts and feelings openly, and listen attentively to your partner's perspective with empathy and understanding.

Find Common Ground: Identify areas of agreement and common ground in your parenting approaches, and build upon these shared values to create a foundation of unity and collaboration.

Seek Compromise: Seek compromise and find creative solutions that honor both partners' parenting styles and preferences. Be willing to meet halfway and find a middle ground that respects each other's perspectives and values.

Finding Harmony

Focus on Shared Goals: Shift the focus of parenting discussions from differences in style to shared goals and values for your children's upbringing. Focus on what you both want for your children's well-being and development, and work together to achieve these goals.

Respect Each Other's Strengths: Recognize and appreciate each other's strengths and contributions as parents. Respect each other's unique perspectives and approaches, and leverage each other's strengths to create a balanced and nurturing environment for your children.

Support Each Other: Support each other in implementing your parenting decisions and strategies, even if they differ from your own preferences. Present a united front to your children, and show them that you are a team working together to support and guide them.

Nurturing Happiness and Understanding

By addressing disagreements over parenting styles with empathy, communication, and a willingness to compromise, couples can fill their lives with happiness and strengthen their love for each other. Here's how:

Deepened Connection: By openly discussing parenting styles and finding common ground, couples can deepen their emotional connection and understanding, fostering a greater sense of unity and partnership in their marriage.

Increased Confidence: By supporting each other in their parenting decisions and strategies, couples can increase their confidence and competence as parents, leading to greater overall happiness and satisfaction in their family life.

Enhanced Communication: Open and honest communication about parenting styles promotes healthy communication habits in the relationship, making it easier to address issues and conflicts constructively.

Strengthened Bond: By working together to harmonize their parenting styles, couples can strengthen their bond and create a supportive and nurturing environment for their children to thrive.

Conclusion

Parenting disagreements are a natural part of marriage, but with understanding, compromise, and effective communication, couples can navigate these challenges and cultivate a harmonious environment for their family. By embracing open dialogue, finding common ground, and supporting each other as parents, couples can fill their lives with happiness, strengthen their bond, and create a loving and nurturing home for their children to grow and flourish. With love and unity as their guiding principles, couples can overcome any parenting challenge and emerge stronger and more connected than ever before.

Embracing Balance: Overcoming the Feeling of Being Overwhelmed

In the whirlwind of marriage, it's not uncommon for life to throw us curveballs that leave us feeling overwhelmed and stretched thin. Whether it's juggling work responsibilities, managing household chores, or dealing with unexpected challenges, the feeling of being overwhelmed can cast a shadow over our lives, affecting our well-being and straining our relationships. But fear not! With a blend of self-care, effective time management, and open communication, couples can navigate through the storm and emerge stronger, happier, and more connected than ever before.

Understanding the Issue

Feeling overwhelmed often stems from a combination of external pressures and internal stressors. From demanding work schedules to family obligations and personal responsibilities, it's easy to feel like we're drowning in a sea of tasks and expectations. This sense of overwhelm can lead to feelings of anxiety, frustration, and burnout, impacting our mental and emotional well-being as well as our relationships.

Embracing Self-Care

Prioritize Self-Care: Make self-care a priority in your daily routine, carving out time for activities that nourish your mind, body, and soul. Whether it's practicing mindfulness, engaging in physical exercise, or indulging in hobbies you enjoy, prioritize activities that replenish your energy and bring you joy.

Set Boundaries: Learn to set boundaries and say no to activities or commitments that drain your energy or add unnecessary stress to your life. Prioritize tasks based on importance and urgency, and delegate responsibilities whenever possible to lighten your load.

Practice Mindfulness: Cultivate mindfulness and present-moment awareness in your daily life, paying attention to your thoughts, feelings, and physical sensations without judgment. Mindfulness can help you manage stress more effectively and respond to challenges with greater clarity and resilience.

Effective Time Management

Create a Schedule: Create a schedule or to-do list to help you prioritize tasks and manage your time more effectively. Break down larger tasks into smaller, more manageable steps, and allocate specific time slots for completing each task.

Focus on One Thing at a Time: Avoid multitasking and focus on one task at a time to maximize productivity and reduce feelings of overwhelm. By focusing your attention on one thing at a time, you can work more efficiently and effectively, ultimately reducing stress and anxiety.

Take Breaks: Remember to take regular breaks throughout the day to rest and recharge. Step away from your work or responsibilities for a few minutes to stretch, take a walk, or engage in relaxation techniques such as deep breathing or meditation.

Open Communication

Share Your Feelings: Share your feelings of overwhelm with your partner in an open and honest manner. Express your concerns and struggles without judgment or blame, and listen empathetically to your partner's perspective.

Work Together: Work together as a team to identify solutions and strategies for managing stress and reducing overwhelm. Brainstorm ideas, set goals, and support each other in implementing changes that promote a healthier and more balanced lifestyle.

Seek Support: Seek support from each other, friends, family members, or a therapist if you're feeling overwhelmed. Sometimes, talking to a trusted confidant or seeking professional help can provide valuable insights and support in navigating challenging times.

Nurturing Happiness and Understanding

By addressing feelings of overwhelm with self-care, effective time management, and open communication, couples can fill their lives with happiness and strengthen their love for each other. Here's how:

Deepened Connection: By sharing their feelings and supporting each other through challenging times, couples can deepen their emotional connection and understanding, fostering a greater sense of intimacy and trust in their relationship.

Increased Resilience: By practicing self-care and effective stress management techniques, couples can increase their resilience and ability to cope with life's challenges, leading to greater overall happiness and well-being.

Enhanced Communication: Open and honest communication about feelings of overwhelm promotes healthy communication habits in the relationship, making it easier to address issues and conflicts constructively.

Strengthened Bond: By working together to overcome feelings of overwhelm, couples can strengthen their bond and create a supportive and nurturing environment where they can weather any storm together.

Conclusion

Feeling overwhelmed is a common challenge in marriage, but with self-care, effective time management, and open communication, couples can navigate through the storm and emerge stronger and more resilient than ever before. By prioritizing their well-being, supporting each other through challenging times, and fostering open communication, couples can fill their lives with happiness, strengthen their bond, and cultivate a love that can weather any storm. With patience, understanding, and a willingness to lean on each other for support, couples can overcome feelings of overwhelm and create a life filled with joy, love, and harmony.

Finding Your Voice: Overcoming the Feeling of Not Being Heard

In marriage, feeling unheard can cast a shadow over the brightest of days. It's a common challenge that many couples face – the feeling that your opinions, thoughts, or feelings are being overlooked or disregarded. But fear not! With patience, empathy, and effective communication, couples can bridge the gap and cultivate a deeper understanding and appreciation for each other's perspectives.

Understanding the Issue

Feeling unheard can stem from a variety of factors, including communication barriers, differences in communication styles, or underlying feelings of neglect or unimportance. It's a deeply personal experience that can lead to feelings of frustration, resentment, and disconnection within the relationship.

Empathetic Listening

Create Space for Listening: Make a conscious effort to create space for listening in your interactions with your partner. Set aside distractions, such as phones or TVs, and give your full attention to your partner when they're speaking.

Practice Active Listening: Practice active listening by giving your partner your full attention, maintaining eye contact, and nodding or providing verbal cues to show that you're engaged and attentive. Reflect back what your partner is saying to ensure understanding and validate their feelings.

Validate Your Partner's Feelings: Validate your partner's feelings by acknowledging their experiences and emotions without judgment or criticism. Let them know that their thoughts and feelings are important to you, and that you're willing to listen and understand.

Expressing Yourself Effectively

Use "I" Statements: Use "I" statements to express your thoughts and feelings in a non-confrontational and constructive manner. Instead of blaming or accusing your partner, focus on sharing your own perspective and experiences.

Be Specific: Be specific and concrete in your communication, articulating exactly what you're feeling or needing in the moment. Avoid vague or general statements that may lead to misunderstanding or confusion.

Express Empathy: Express empathy towards your partner's perspective, even if you disagree with their point of view. Show that you understand and respect their feelings, and be open to finding common ground or compromise.

Creating a Safe Environment for Communication

Set Aside Time for Communication: Set aside dedicated time for open and honest communication with your partner. Create a safe and supportive environment where both partners feel comfortable expressing their thoughts, feelings, and concerns.

Practice Non-Defensive Communication: Practice non-defensive communication by avoiding criticism, defensiveness, contempt, or stonewalling during discussions. Instead, focus on active listening, empathy, and mutual respect.

Seek Professional Help: If communication challenges persist despite your best efforts, consider seeking professional help from a couples therapist or counselor. A trained professional can provide guidance, support, and tools for improving communication and resolving conflicts.

Nurturing Happiness and Understanding

By addressing feelings of being unheard with empathy, effective communication, and a willingness to understand each other's perspectives, couples can fill their lives with happiness and strengthen their love for each other. Here's how:

Deepened Connection: By practicing empathetic listening and expressing themselves effectively, couples can deepen their emotional connection and understanding, fostering a greater sense of intimacy and trust in their relationship.

Increased Mutual Respect: By creating a safe environment for communication and practicing non-defensive communication, couples can increase their mutual respect and appreciation for each other's perspectives, leading to greater overall happiness and harmony in their relationship.

Enhanced Communication Skills: Open and honest communication about feelings of being unheard promotes healthy communication habits in the relationship, making it easier to address issues and conflicts constructively.

Strengthened Bond: By working together to overcome feelings of being unheard, couples can strengthen their bond and create a supportive and nurturing environment where they can communicate openly and authentically with each other.

Conclusion

Feeling unheard is a common challenge in marriage, but with patience, empathy, and effective communication, couples can bridge the gap and cultivate a deeper understanding and appreciation for each other's perspectives. By practicing empathetic listening, expressing themselves effectively, and creating a safe environment for communication, couples can fill their lives with happiness, strengthen their bond, and create a love that truly listens and understands. With love and understanding as their guiding principles, couples can overcome any challenge and emerge stronger and more connected than ever before.

Navigating Health Challenges: Strengthening Your Relationship Through Adversity

In the journey of marriage, facing health problems can be like navigating stormy seas. Whether it's coping with chronic illness, managing unexpected medical emergencies, or supporting each other through physical and mental health struggles, health issues can place extra strain on a relationship. However, with patience, resilience, and a shared commitment to support each other, couples can weather the storm and emerge stronger, closer, and more resilient than ever before.

Understanding the Issue

Health problems can vary widely in their nature and severity, ranging from minor ailments to chronic conditions or life-threatening illnesses. Regardless of the specific health issue, the impact on a relationship can be profound. It can disrupt daily routines, challenge emotional resilience, and create financial burdens, leading to increased stress and strain on the couple's relationship.

Supporting Each Other

Open Communication: Create a safe space for open and honest communication about your health concerns, fears, and needs. Share your thoughts and feelings with your partner, and listen attentively to their concerns and perspectives without judgment or criticism.

Offer Emotional Support: Offer emotional support to your partner by validating their feelings, providing reassurance, and expressing empathy and understanding. Be a source of comfort and strength for each other, offering a shoulder to lean on during difficult times.

Practical Assistance: Offer practical assistance to your partner, such as helping with household chores, running errands, or accompanying them to medical appointments. By sharing the burden of caregiving responsibilities, you can lighten each other's load and strengthen your bond as a couple.

Coping Strategies

Seek Professional Help: Seek professional help from healthcare providers, therapists, or support groups to help you cope with your health challenges. Professional guidance and support can provide valuable insights, coping strategies, and resources to help you navigate through difficult times.

Practice Self-Care: Prioritize self-care and prioritize your physical, emotional, and mental well-being. Engage in activities that nourish your mind, body, and soul, such as exercise, meditation, hobbies, or spending time with loved ones.

Focus on the Positive: Focus on the positive aspects of your relationship and your life together, even in the face of adversity. Celebrate small victories, cherish moments of joy and connection, and maintain a hopeful outlook for the future.

Nurturing Happiness and Understanding

By supporting each other through health challenges with patience, resilience, and empathy, couples can fill their lives with happiness and strengthen their love for each other. Here's how:

Deepened Empathy: By experiencing health challenges together, couples can deepen their empathy and understanding for each other's experiences, feelings, and needs. This shared journey of adversity can foster a deeper emotional connection and intimacy in the relationship.

Increased Resilience: By facing health challenges as a team, couples can increase their resilience and ability to cope with adversity. By supporting each other through difficult times, couples can emerge stronger, more resilient, and more united than ever before.

Enhanced Appreciation: By navigating health challenges together, couples can develop a deeper appreciation for the strength, resilience, and love that they share. This shared experience can deepen their gratitude for each other and reinforce their commitment to supporting each other through thick and thin.

Strengthened Bond: By supporting each other through health challenges, couples can strengthen their bond and create a deeper sense of trust, intimacy, and connection in their relationship. By facing adversity together, couples can emerge stronger, closer, and more united than ever before.

Conclusion

While facing health problems can pose challenges to a relationship, with patience, resilience, and a shared commitment to support each other, couples can navigate through difficult times and emerge stronger, closer, and more resilient than ever before. By supporting each other emotionally, offering practical assistance, and seeking professional help when needed, couples can weather the storm of health challenges and create a life filled with happiness, understanding, and love. With love and compassion as their guiding principles, couples can overcome any obstacle and emerge stronger, closer, and more connected than ever before.

Addressing Baggage from the Past: Building a Stronger Future Together

In the journey of marriage, unresolved past issues can linger like shadows, casting doubt and discord on the present. Whether it's old wounds from previous relationships, childhood traumas, or unresolved conflicts with family members, the baggage we carry from the past can weigh heavily on our present relationships. But fret not! With patience, understanding, and a willingness to confront and heal from the past, couples can pave the way for a brighter, more fulfilling future together.

Understanding the Issue

Unresolved past issues can manifest in various ways within a relationship, including trust issues, communication barriers, or repeated patterns of conflict. These unresolved issues may stem from previous experiences of betrayal, abandonment, or neglect, leaving emotional scars that impact our ability to trust, communicate, and connect with our partner in the present.

Acknowledging the Past

Open Dialogue: Create a safe space for open and honest dialogue about past experiences and their impact on your relationship. Encourage your partner to share their thoughts, feelings, and concerns without fear of judgment or reprisal.

Validate Feelings: Validate your partner's feelings and experiences by acknowledging the significance of their past struggles and the impact they may have had on their present outlook and behavior. Express empathy and understanding, and reassure your partner that their feelings are valid and worthy of consideration.

Practice Active Listening: Practice active listening by giving your partner your full attention, maintaining eye contact, and reflecting back what you hear to ensure understanding. Avoid interrupting or jumping to conclusions, and allow your partner the space to express themselves fully.

Healing and Moving Forward

Seek Closure: Seek closure for unresolved past issues by addressing them directly with your partner. Engage in open and honest conversations about past hurts, grievances, and misunderstandings, and work together to find resolution and closure.

Forgiveness: Practice forgiveness as a means of releasing the grip of the past and moving forward with a clean slate. This doesn't mean condoning or excusing past actions, but rather choosing to let go of resentment and anger in order to free yourself from the burden of carrying grudges.

Therapeutic Support: Consider seeking therapeutic support from a couples therapist or counselor to help navigate through unresolved past issues. A trained professional can provide guidance, support, and tools for addressing past traumas and building a stronger, more resilient relationship.

Nurturing Happiness and Understanding

By addressing unresolved past issues with empathy, understanding, and a commitment to healing, couples can fill their lives with happiness and strengthen their love for each other. Here's how:

Deepened Empathy: By acknowledging and validating each other's past experiences and struggles, couples can deepen their empathy and understanding for each other's perspectives, fostering a greater sense of emotional connection and intimacy.

Increased Trust: By confronting unresolved past issues head-on and working through them together, couples can rebuild trust and strengthen the foundation of their relationship. This renewed sense of trust can create a safe and secure space for open and honest communication and deepen their bond as a couple.

Enhanced Communication: By practicing open and honest communication about past issues, couples can develop healthier communication patterns and gain insight into each other's thoughts, feelings, and needs. This improved communication can strengthen their connection and pave the way for a more harmonious and fulfilling relationship.

Strengthened Resilience: By confronting and healing from unresolved past issues, couples can increase their resilience and ability to overcome challenges together. This shared journey of healing can deepen their bond and empower them to face future obstacles with courage, compassion, and a sense of unity.

Conclusion

While confronting unresolved past issues may be daunting, with patience, understanding, and a willingness to heal, couples can pave the way for a brighter, more fulfilling future together. By acknowledging the impact of the past on their present relationship, practicing open and honest communication, and seeking support when needed, couples can heal from past wounds and build a stronger, more resilient foundation for their relationship. With love, compassion, and a shared commitment to growth and healing, couples can overcome the shadows of the past and embrace the possibilities of a brighter tomorrow.

Bridging the Emotional Gap: Strengthening Your Connection

In marriage, emotional distance can feel like a chasm separating two hearts. It's that gnawing sensation that despite physical proximity, there's a vast expanse between you and your partner emotionally. But fear not! With patience, understanding, and a commitment to reconnecting, couples can bridge the emotional gap and cultivate a deeper, more fulfilling connection.

Understanding the Issue

Emotional distance can manifest in various ways within a relationship, such as feeling disconnected, misunderstood, or unable to express oneself authentically. It may stem from factors like communication barriers, unresolved conflicts, or individual emotional baggage. Regardless of the underlying cause, the impact is often a sense of loneliness, frustration, and dissatisfaction within the relationship.

Creating Emotional Intimacy

Open Communication: Foster open and honest communication by creating a safe space where both partners feel comfortable expressing their thoughts, feelings, and needs without fear of judgment or rejection. Take the time to actively listen to each other's concerns and validate each other's experiences.

Share Vulnerabilities: Practice vulnerability by sharing your innermost thoughts, fears, and insecurities with your partner. By allowing yourselves to be seen and accepted for who you truly are, you can deepen your emotional connection and foster a greater sense of intimacy.

Express Appreciation: Show appreciation for your partner's efforts, qualities, and contributions to the relationship. Express gratitude for the little things they do, and make an effort to acknowledge their value and importance in your life on a regular basis.

Reconnecting with Your Partner

Quality Time Together: Make quality time together a priority in your relationship. Set aside dedicated time for shared activities, conversations, and experiences that bring you closer together and foster a deeper sense of connection.

Physical Touch: Physical touch is a powerful way to express love and affection, and it can help bridge the emotional gap between partners. Make an effort to incorporate physical affection into your daily interactions, whether it's holding hands, hugging, or cuddling.

Shared Goals and Dreams: Identify shared goals, dreams, and aspirations as a couple, and work together towards achieving them. By aligning your visions for the future and supporting each other's growth and development, you can strengthen your bond and deepen your emotional connection.

Healing Past Wounds

Forgiveness: Practice forgiveness as a means of releasing past hurts and resentments. Let go of grudges and grievances, and choose to forgive your partner for any past mistakes or transgressions. By offering forgiveness, you free yourself from the burden of carrying negative emotions and open the door to healing and reconciliation.

Seeking Closure: Seek closure for unresolved conflicts or issues from the past by addressing them directly with your partner. Engage in open and honest conversations about past hurts, and work together to find resolution and closure.

Therapeutic Support: Consider seeking therapeutic support from a couples therapist or counselor to help navigate through unresolved emotional issues. A trained professional can provide guidance, support, and tools for addressing past wounds and rebuilding trust and intimacy in the relationship.

Nurturing Happiness and Understanding

By bridging the emotional gap with patience, understanding, and a commitment to reconnecting, couples can fill their lives with happiness and strengthen their love for each other. Here's how:

Deepened Connection: By fostering open communication, vulnerability, and shared experiences, couples can deepen their emotional connection and intimacy, leading to greater overall happiness and satisfaction in the relationship.

Increased Understanding: By actively listening to each other's concerns and perspectives and practicing empathy and validation, couples can gain a deeper understanding of each other's needs and feelings, fostering a greater sense of mutual understanding and support.

Enhanced Trust: By addressing past wounds and conflicts with forgiveness, closure, and therapeutic support, couples can rebuild trust and confidence in the relationship, creating a solid foundation for future growth and happiness together.

Strengthened Bond: By committing to bridging the emotional gap and reconnecting with each other on a deeper level, couples can strengthen their bond and create a more resilient, fulfilling relationship that stands the test of time.

Conclusion

While navigating emotional distance in a relationship may feel daunting, with patience, understanding, and a commitment to reconnecting, couples can bridge the gap and cultivate a deeper, more fulfilling connection. By fostering open communication, vulnerability, and shared experiences, addressing past wounds with forgiveness and closure, and seeking therapeutic support when needed, couples can fill their lives with happiness and strengthen their love for each other. With love, compassion, and a shared commitment to growth and connection, couples can overcome any obstacle and emerge stronger, closer, and more connected than ever before.

Embracing Differences: Finding Harmony in Varied Interests

In the beautiful symphony of marriage, sometimes the notes of our interests and hobbies don't quite harmonize. It's like trying to dance to different rhythms – while one partner may sway to the beat of sports or outdoor adventures, the other might find solace in the melody of books or art. But fear not! With a little creativity, compromise, and open-mindedness, couples can turn their diverse interests into a delightful duet that enriches their relationship and strengthens their bond.

Understanding the Issue

Divergent interests and hobbies can create a sense of disconnection and frustration within a relationship. It's natural for individuals to have their own passions and pursuits, but when these interests clash or leave little room for shared activities, it can lead to feelings of loneliness and disconnect. Finding common ground amidst these differences is key to nurturing a fulfilling and harmonious partnership.

Embracing Diversity

Open Communication: Start by openly discussing your interests and hobbies with your partner. Share what brings you joy and fulfillment, and listen attentively as your partner does the same. This creates a foundation of understanding and respect for each other's individual passions.

Explore Each Other's Worlds: Take the opportunity to explore each other's interests and hobbies. Attend events, try new activities, or simply spend time together while engaging in your partner's favorite pastime. This not only allows you to better understand each other but also fosters a sense of closeness and connection.

Find Common Ground: Identify activities or interests that you both enjoy or are willing to try. Whether it's cooking together, hiking in nature, or even binge-watching a favorite TV show, finding shared experiences strengthens your bond and creates lasting memories.

Compromise and Flexibility

Rotate Activities: Create a balance by rotating activities that cater to each other's interests. Designate specific days or weekends for pursuing individual hobbies, and set aside time for shared activities that both partners can enjoy together.

Support Each Other: Show genuine interest and support for your partner's hobbies, even if they differ from your own. Attend their events, cheer them on, and celebrate their achievements. This demonstrates your commitment to their happiness and strengthens your bond as a couple.

Be Open to New Experiences: Stay open-minded and be willing to step out of your comfort zone. You may discover new interests or hobbies that you never considered before, enriching your life and broadening your horizons as a couple.

Filling Your Life with Happiness

Celebrate Differences: Instead of viewing diverse interests as obstacles, celebrate them as opportunities for growth and learning. Embrace the uniqueness of each other's passions, and appreciate the richness they bring to your relationship.

Quality Time Together: Prioritize quality time together, regardless of the activity. Whether it's a shared hobby or simply enjoying each other's company, the key is to nurture your connection and strengthen your bond through meaningful interactions.

Laugh Together: Don't forget to inject a healthy dose of humor into your relationship. Find joy in the moments you share, laugh at the quirks and idiosyncrasies of your differences, and revel in the joy of simply being together.

Create New Traditions: Establish your own traditions and rituals that reflect both partners' interests and values. Whether it's a weekly game night, a monthly cooking challenge, or an annual adventure, these shared experiences create a sense of belonging and unity within your relationship.

Understanding and Love

By embracing each other's differences, cultivating a spirit of compromise and flexibility, and prioritizing shared experiences, couples can fill their lives with happiness and strengthen their love for each other. Here's how:

Deepened Connection: By actively engaging in each other's interests and hobbies, couples deepen their understanding and appreciation for one another, fostering a deeper sense of connection and intimacy.

Increased Appreciation: By celebrating each other's passions and supporting one another's pursuits, couples demonstrate their love and appreciation for each other's individuality, strengthening their bond and creating a more harmonious relationship.

Enhanced Communication: By openly discussing their interests and hobbies and finding ways to incorporate them into their relationship, couples improve their communication and problem-solving skills, fostering a more collaborative and resilient partnership.

Strengthened Bond: By prioritizing shared experiences and creating new traditions together, couples strengthen their bond and create lasting memories that deepen their love and commitment to each other.

Conclusion

While navigating different interests and hobbies in a relationship may present its challenges, with patience, understanding, and a willingness to compromise, couples can turn these differences into opportunities for growth and connection. By embracing each other's passions, supporting one another's pursuits, and prioritizing shared experiences, couples can fill their lives with happiness and deepen their love and understanding for each other. With love, respect, and a spirit of adventure, every difference becomes a delightful discovery, and every challenge becomes an opportunity for growth and connection.

Navigating Social Expectations: Crafting Your Own Relationship Path

In the whirlwind of life, it's easy to feel swept away by the currents of social pressures and expectations, especially when it comes to relationships. Whether it's pressure from family, friends, or society at large, these external influences can cast a shadow over the unique bond between partners. But fear not! By staying true to yourselves, communicating openly, and setting boundaries, couples can rise above the noise and forge a path that brings them joy, fulfillment, and mutual understanding.

Understanding the Issue

Social pressures can manifest in various forms, from subtle comments about when to get married or have children to overt judgments about the dynamics of your relationship. These pressures can create feelings of doubt, insecurity, and inadequacy, as couples grapple with the expectations imposed upon them by others.

Staying True to Yourselves

Define Your Priorities: Take the time to reflect on what truly matters to you and your partner. Identify your shared values, goals, and aspirations, and use these as guiding principles for your relationship. By aligning your priorities, you can confidently navigate external pressures without losing sight of what's important to you as a couple.

Communicate Openly: Foster open and honest communication with your partner about your feelings regarding social pressures. Share your concerns, fears, and insecurities, and listen empathetically as your partner does the same. By validating each other's experiences, you can provide much-needed support and reassurance in the face of external scrutiny.

Set Boundaries: Establish clear boundaries with friends, family, and society regarding your relationship. Communicate assertively but respectfully about what is and isn't acceptable in terms of their involvement or opinions. By asserting your autonomy as a couple, you can create a safe space where your relationship can flourish free from external interference.

Navigating External Influences

Cultivate Supportive Relationships: Surround yourselves with friends and family who respect and support your relationship. Seek out mentors or couples who have successfully navigated similar challenges and draw inspiration from their experiences. Having a strong support system can provide encouragement and validation during times of doubt or uncertainty.

Educate Others: Take the opportunity to educate friends, family, and society at large about the diverse nature of relationships. Challenge stereotypes and misconceptions by sharing your own story and highlighting the unique strengths and dynamics of your partnership. By promoting understanding and acceptance, you can help create a more inclusive and supportive environment for all couples.

Focus on Your Journey: Remember that your relationship is yours and yours alone. Resist the temptation to compare yourselves to others or conform to societal norms that don't align with your values. Instead, focus on nurturing your connection, fostering mutual respect, and building a life together that brings you joy and fulfillment.

Filling Your Life with Happiness

Celebrate Your Unique Bond: Embrace the uniqueness of your relationship and celebrate the qualities that make it special. Whether it's shared inside jokes, common interests, or shared goals, cherish the moments that bring you closer together and reinforce your bond as a couple.

Practice Gratitude: Cultivate a sense of gratitude for the love and support you receive from your partner. Take the time to express appreciation for the little things they do, and make an effort to acknowledge their efforts and sacrifices in nurturing your relationship.

Prioritize Self-Care: Take care of yourselves individually and as a couple by prioritizing self-care and well-being. Make time for activities that bring you joy and relaxation, whether it's exercise, hobbies, or spending quality time together.

By nurturing yourselves, you can strengthen your relationship and better withstand external pressures.

Seek Professional Help if Needed: If social pressures are causing significant distress or strain on your relationship, don't hesitate to seek professional help. A qualified therapist or counselor can provide guidance, support, and tools for navigating external influences and strengthening your bond as a couple.

Conclusion

While social pressures may create challenges in a relationship, with open communication, assertiveness, and a focus on authenticity, couples can rise above external expectations and forge a path that brings them happiness and fulfillment. By staying true to themselves, cultivating supportive relationships, and prioritizing their bond, couples can navigate external pressures with confidence and create a relationship that is uniquely their own. Remember, your love story is yours to write – so embrace it with pride, resilience, and a sense of adventure.

Untangling the Web: Navigating Technology Distractions in Relationships

In today's digital age, technology has become an integral part of our daily lives, often blurring the lines between virtual and real-world interactions. While smartphones and devices have revolutionized communication and connectivity, they also pose a significant challenge for couples trying to maintain meaningful connections in their relationship. The incessant ping of notifications, the lure of social media scrolling, and the temptation to escape into the digital realm can all contribute to a sense of disconnection and dissatisfaction within a partnership. But fear not! By setting boundaries, prioritizing quality time, and fostering open communication, couples can reclaim their connection and rediscover the joy of being present with each other.

Understanding the Issue

Technology distractions can manifest in various forms, from compulsive smartphone checking during meals to zoning out on social media instead of engaging in meaningful conversation. These distractions not only detract from the quality of interactions between partners but also create feelings of neglect, frustration, and loneliness. In a world where screens vie for our attention at every turn, finding a balance between digital and real-world connections is essential for nurturing a thriving relationship.

Setting Boundaries

Establish Tech-Free Zones: Designate specific times or areas in your home where devices are off-limits. Whether it's during meals, bedtime, or designated "date nights," creating tech-free zones fosters an environment where you can focus on each other without the distractions of screens and notifications.

Create Digital Detox Days: Schedule regular digital detox days where you and your partner disconnect from screens and engage in offline activities together. Whether it's going for a nature walk, cooking a meal together, or playing board games, these tech-free days provide an opportunity to reconnect and rediscover the joy of shared experiences.

Set Screen Time Limits: Utilize built-in screen time tracking features or third-party apps to set limits on your device usage. Establishing boundaries around screen time encourages mindful usage and prevents technology from encroaching on quality time with your partner.

Prioritizing Quality Time

Plan Meaningful Activities: Make a conscious effort to plan activities that encourage quality time and meaningful interaction. Whether it's trying a new hobby together, exploring a new neighborhood, or simply enjoying a quiet evening at home, prioritize experiences that strengthen your bond and create lasting memories.

Practice Active Listening: Put down your devices and actively listen to your partner when they speak. Show genuine interest in their thoughts, feelings, and experiences, and refrain from multitasking or distracted listening. By giving each other your full attention, you demonstrate respect and appreciation for your partner's presence.

Schedule Regular Check-Ins: Set aside time for regular check-ins to discuss your relationship and address any concerns or issues that may arise. Use this dedicated time to express gratitude, share your thoughts and feelings, and reaffirm your commitment to each other. Open communication is key to maintaining a strong and healthy relationship in the digital age.

Fostering Open Communication

Express Your Needs: Communicate openly with your partner about how technology distractions impact your relationship. Share your concerns, feelings, and preferences regarding device usage, and listen empathetically as your partner does the same. By expressing your needs and concerns, you can work together to find mutually agreeable solutions.

Establish Shared Rules: Collaborate with your partner to establish shared rules and guidelines around device usage in your relationship. Discuss what behaviors are acceptable and unacceptable, and agree on strategies for minimizing distractions and prioritizing quality time together.

Lead by Example: Be mindful of your own device usage and lead by example in your relationship. Set boundaries for yourself, practice self-discipline, and prioritize face-to-face interactions over virtual connections. By modeling healthy device habits, you create a positive environment that encourages mutual respect and connection.

Filling Your Life with Happiness

Reconnect with Nature: Spend time outdoors together, enjoying the beauty of nature and the simple pleasures of being present in the moment. Whether it's going for a hike, having a picnic in the park, or stargazing on a clear night, reconnecting with nature can rejuvenate your relationship and fill your life with happiness.

Cultivate Shared Interests: Discover new hobbies or interests that you can pursue together as a couple. Whether it's cooking, gardening, or learning a new language, cultivating shared interests strengthens your bond and provides opportunities for growth and connection.

Celebrate Small Moments: Take time to celebrate the small moments of joy and connection in your relationship. Whether it's sharing a laugh, enjoying a quiet moment together, or expressing gratitude for each other's presence, these small gestures of love and appreciation add up to create a life filled with happiness and love.

Conclusion

While technology distractions may pose challenges for couples in today's digital age, with mindful awareness, open communication, and a commitment to prioritizing quality time together, couples can overcome these obstacles and strengthen their connection. By setting boundaries, fostering open communication, and prioritizing meaningful interactions, couples can reclaim their relationship from the grip of technology and rediscover the joy of being present with each other. Remember, the key to a thriving relationship lies not in the number of likes or notifications but in the depth of connection and intimacy you share with your partner.

Rediscovering Yourself: Navigating Loss of Identity in Relationships

Imagine feeling like you've lost sight of who you are, like your individuality has somehow become overshadowed by the dynamics of your relationship. It's a common challenge that many couples face—the loss of identity. When your sense of self becomes entwined with your partner's, it can lead to feelings of confusion, dissatisfaction, and even resentment. But fear not, for reclaiming your identity and reigniting your sense of self is entirely possible. By embarking on a journey of self-discovery, setting boundaries, and prioritizing self-care, you can reconnect with the person you were before the relationship and cultivate a deeper sense of fulfillment and happiness.

Understanding the Issue

Losing your identity within a relationship can happen gradually, often without you even realizing it. Perhaps you've been so focused on nurturing your partnership or accommodating your partner's needs that you've neglected your own interests, passions, and desires. Over time, this can lead to a sense of disconnection from yourself, leaving you feeling adrift and unfulfilled.

Embarking on a Journey of Self-Discovery

Reflect on Your Passions: Take some time to reflect on the things that truly bring you joy and fulfillment. What activities did you enjoy before the relationship? What are your hobbies, interests, and passions? Reconnecting with these aspects of yourself can reignite your sense of purpose and identity.

Set Personal Goals: Establishing personal goals and aspirations can help you regain a sense of direction and purpose outside of the relationship. Whether it's pursuing further education, starting a new hobby, or focusing on your career, setting goals allows you to invest in your personal growth and development.

Explore New Opportunities: Be open to exploring new experiences and opportunities that pique your interest. Step outside of your comfort zone and embrace the unknown. Trying new things can broaden your horizons, boost your confidence, and help you discover new facets of yourself.

Setting Boundaries

Establish Individual Time: Make it a priority to carve out time for yourself, separate from your partner. Whether it's taking a solo walk, indulging in a hobby, or simply enjoying some quiet time alone, setting aside moments for self-reflection and rejuvenation is essential for maintaining a healthy sense of self.

Communicate Your Needs: Be open and honest with your partner about your need for space and individuality. Communicate your boundaries respectfully and assertively, emphasizing the importance of self-care and personal growth in maintaining a strong and fulfilling relationship.

Respect Each Other's Independence: Encourage each other to pursue individual interests and passions, even if they differ from your own. Respect each other's autonomy and support each other's pursuits, knowing that fostering independence strengthens the bond between you.

Prioritizing Self-Care

Practice Mindfulness: Cultivate mindfulness practices such as meditation, yoga, or deep breathing exercises to center yourself and cultivate self-awareness. Being present in the moment allows you to connect with your inner self and tune into your thoughts, feelings, and emotions.

Nurture Your Well-Being: Prioritize self-care activities that nourish your mind, body, and soul. Whether it's getting enough sleep, eating nutritious foods, exercising regularly, or indulging in creative outlets, taking care of your well-being is essential for maintaining a strong sense of self.

Seek Support: Don't hesitate to seek support from friends, family, or a therapist if you're struggling to reclaim your identity. Surround yourself with a supportive network of individuals who encourage you to be true to yourself and pursue your passions.

Filling Your Life with Happiness

Celebrate Your Individuality: Embrace your uniqueness and celebrate the qualities that make you who you are. Recognize that your individuality enriches your relationship and contributes to its vibrancy and depth.

Find Joy in Shared Moments: While it's important to prioritize your individuality, don't overlook the joy of shared experiences with your partner. Celebrate the moments of connection, intimacy, and laughter that strengthen your bond and bring you closer together.

Stay True to Yourself: Above all, stay true to yourself and honor your authentic desires, values, and aspirations. Remember that your identity is a valuable and integral part of who you are, and embracing it fully allows you to live a life filled with happiness, fulfillment, and love.

In essence, reclaiming your identity is a journey of self-discovery and self-empowerment. By prioritizing self-care, setting boundaries, and nurturing your individuality, you can rediscover the essence of who you are and cultivate a deeper sense of happiness and fulfillment within yourself and your relationship.

Sharing the Load: Navigating Household Chores in Your Relationship

Let's talk about household chores—the not-so-glamorous but oh-so-necessary tasks that keep our homes running smoothly. From doing the dishes to folding laundry, figuring out who does what around the house can sometimes lead to disagreements and tension between partners. But fear not, because with some communication, compromise, and teamwork, you can tackle household chores together and create a harmonious living environment that fosters love and understanding.

Understanding the Issue

Household chores may seem like a mundane aspect of daily life, but they can have a significant impact on the dynamics of your relationship. When one partner feels like they're carrying the brunt of the workload while the other seems oblivious or indifferent, resentment can start to build. It's not just about dirty dishes or piles of laundry—it's about feeling valued, respected, and supported in your shared responsibilities.

Communicate Openly and Honestly

Initiate a Conversation: Sit down with your partner and initiate an open and honest conversation about household chores. Express your feelings and concerns calmly and respectfully, emphasizing the importance of working together as a team to maintain a clean and organized home.

Identify Individual Preferences: Take the time to discuss each other's preferences and strengths when it comes to household tasks. Maybe one of you enjoys cooking while the other prefers doing the laundry. By understanding each other's preferences, you can divide chores in a way that feels fair and balanced.

Create a Chore Schedule: Establish a chore schedule that outlines specific tasks and responsibilities for each partner. Be flexible and willing to adjust the schedule as needed to accommodate changes in your routines or commitments.

Practice Empathy and Understanding

Acknowledge Each Other's Efforts: Take the time to acknowledge and appreciate each other's contributions to the household. Whether it's a simple "thank you" for doing the dishes or a heartfelt expression of gratitude for tackling a particularly challenging task, showing appreciation goes a long way in fostering mutual respect and understanding.

Be Empathetic: Recognize that everyone has their own strengths, limitations, and preferences when it comes to household chores. Instead of focusing on what your partner isn't doing, focus on what they are doing and offer support and encouragement when needed.

Work as a Team: Approach household chores as a team effort rather than individual responsibilities. When you work together towards a common goal, you not only lighten the load but also strengthen your bond as partners.

Find Creative Solutions

Divide and Conquer: Divide household chores based on each partner's preferences, strengths, and availability. Maybe one of you takes on more indoor chores while the other handles outdoor tasks, or perhaps you alternate responsibilities on a weekly basis. Find a system that works for both of you.

Outsource When Necessary: Don't hesitate to outsource certain tasks if you have the means to do so. Whether it's hiring a cleaning service to deep clean your home once a month or ordering takeout on busy nights, outsourcing can alleviate stress and free up time for more meaningful activities together.

Make It Fun: Turn household chores into a bonding experience by making them more enjoyable. Put on some music and dance while you clean, turn laundry folding into a game, or cook a meal together as a team. Finding joy in the process can make chores feel less like a chore and more like a shared adventure.

Prioritize Quality Time Together

Set Aside Dedicated Time: Make sure to set aside dedicated time for quality time together amidst your busy schedules. Whether it's a weekly date night or a cozy evening at home, prioritize spending meaningful time together to strengthen your connection and reinforce your bond.

Communicate Regularly: Keep the lines of communication open and check in with each other regularly to ensure that both partners feel heard, valued, and supported. Address any concerns or issues as they arise, and work together to find constructive solutions.

Celebrate Your Achievements: Celebrate your achievements, both big and small, as you navigate household chores together. Whether it's conquering a particularly daunting task or simply maintaining a clean and organized home, take the time to acknowledge your accomplishments and celebrate your success as a team.

In essence, tackling household chores together is not just about keeping your home clean and organized—it's about fostering teamwork, communication, and mutual respect in your relationship. By approaching chores with empathy, understanding, and creativity, you can create a harmonious living environment that strengthens your bond and fills your life with happiness and love.